Grandpa's Story

This book belongs to:

_____

_____

Grandpa's Family Tree

Great
Grandfather

Great
Grandmother

Great
Grandfather

Great
Grandmother

Great
Grandfather

Great
Grandmother

Great
Grandfather

Great
Grandmother

Grandfather

Grandmother

Grandfather

Grandmother

Grandpa's Dad

Grandpa's Mom

Grandpa

Grandma

I was born in...

I went to school in...

My best friend's name was...

The best vacation I had was...

_____

_____

_____

_____

_____

_____

_____

_____

_____

_____

_____

_____

_____

_____

_____

_____

_____

_____

Favorite food...

My cousins...

My aunts and uncles...

Places you liked growing up...

_____

_____

_____

_____

_____

_____

_____

_____

_____

_____

_____

_____

_____

_____

_____

_____

_____

_____

_____

Favorite recipe from my childhood...

_____

_____

_____

_____

_____

_____

_____

_____

_____

_____

_____

_____

_____

_____

_____

_____

Favorite subject in school...

My favorite sports growing up was...

What was your neighborhood like?

Memories of my childhood best friend...

Thing I miss the most about being a kid...

_____

_____

_____

_____

_____

_____

_____

_____

_____

_____

_____

_____

_____

_____

_____

_____

_____

_____

My sister(s) name ...

The best memories with her was...

Thing I miss the most about playing with her...

My brother(s) name...

_____
_____
_____
_____
_____
_____
_____
_____
_____
_____
_____
_____
_____
_____
_____
_____
_____
_____

What I most love about him...

Best memory with him...

My mom's name...

_____

_____

_____

_____

_____

_____

_____

_____

_____

_____

_____

_____

_____

_____

_____

_____

_____

_____

My mom was born in...

_____

_____

_____

_____

_____

_____

_____

_____

_____

_____

_____

_____

_____

_____

_____

_____

_____

_____

_____

My favorite memory of her...

Things that she used to tell me...

My dad's name...

_____

_____

_____

_____

_____

_____

_____

_____

_____

_____

_____

_____

_____

_____

_____

_____

_____

He was born in...

Favorite memory of my dad...

I loved when he used to ...

My Grandma's name was...

Things I remember about my grandma...

My Grandpa's name was...

_____

_____

_____

_____

_____

_____

_____

_____

_____

_____

_____

_____

_____

_____

_____

_____

_____

_____

Things I remember about my grandpa...

My pet's name was...

School memories...

My favorite show on TV was...

Now I like to watch...

_____
_____
_____
_____
_____
_____
_____
_____
_____
_____
_____
_____
_____
_____
_____
_____
_____
_____
_____

What did you want to be when you grow up...

Now, my favorite activity is...

The best place i traveled...

A place i would love to live...

A place I would love to travel...

My favorite job was...

_____

_____

_____

_____

_____

_____

_____

_____

_____

_____

_____

_____

_____

_____

_____

_____

_____

_____

Favorite memories of being a dad...

_____

_____

_____

_____

_____

_____

_____

_____

_____

_____

_____

_____

_____

_____

_____

_____

_____

_____

Favorite memory of being a grandpa...

I am thankful for...

_____
_____
_____
_____
_____
_____
_____
_____
_____
_____
_____
_____
_____
_____
_____
_____
_____
_____
_____

My secret for happiness is...

_____

_____

_____

_____

_____

_____

_____

_____

_____

_____

_____

_____

_____

_____

_____

_____

_____

_____

Any advice for your grandsons and granddaughters?

_____

_____

_____

_____

_____

_____

_____

_____

_____

_____

_____

_____

_____

_____

_____

_____

Did you get an allowance?

Did you ever get in trouble as a child or teenager

What was your first car?

Where have you lived? Tell me about your first house

What is your favorite city to visit?

_____

_____

_____

_____

_____

_____

_____

_____

_____

_____

_____

_____

_____

_____

_____

_____

_____

Do you practice a religion?

What is your favorite memory with your children?

How do you handle stress?

What is your dream for your children and grandchildren?

_____

_____

_____

_____

_____

_____

_____

_____

_____

_____

_____

_____

_____

_____

_____

_____

_____

What is the earliest memory that you have?

Tell me about the day when my mom/dad was born?

What makes you happy?

What is different about growing up today than when you were a child?

Do you have a nickname that your siblings or friends call you?

_____

_____

_____

_____

_____

_____

_____

_____

_____

_____

_____

_____

_____

_____

_____

_____

_____

_____

_____

How did you meet Grandfather?

_____

_____

_____

_____

_____

_____

_____

_____

_____

_____

_____

_____

_____

_____

_____

_____

_____

_____

How did you propose to grandma?

_____

_____

_____

_____

_____

_____

_____

_____

_____

_____

_____

_____

_____

_____

_____

_____

_____

When and where were you married?

_____

_____

_____

_____

_____

_____

_____

_____

_____

_____

_____

_____

_____

_____

_____

_____

What are your children's names, and when and where were they born?

Where have you lived?

_____

_____

_____

_____

_____

_____

_____

_____

_____

_____

_____

_____

_____

_____

_____

_____

_____

_____

Has faith or religion played a role in your life?

What did you do to get through the difficult times in your life?

What are your favorite holiday memories and traditions?

What are some of your favorite things?

What experiences in your life have molded you into the person you are today?

What are your favorite things to do now?

What is your medical and genetic history?

How have you served your country?

_____

_____

_____

_____

_____

_____

_____

_____

_____

_____

_____

_____

_____

_____

_____

_____

_____

_____

Do you have any unrealized dreams?

What did you do when you were a teen?

What do you see as your legacy? How did you celebrate the holidays?

How has the world changed since you were my age?

What was my mom or dad like when they were young?

What traditions do you most want our family to continue?

What has your work life been like? What
countries do our people come from?

What role has money played in your life?

_____

_____

_____

_____

_____

_____

_____

_____

_____

_____

_____

_____

_____

_____

_____

_____

_____

_____

_____

Do you remember your first kiss?

Are you the keeper of our family's secrets?

What's the one thing you would do differently?

What are your goals for the future?

Notes

Notes

Notes

Notes

Notes

Notes

Notes

Notes

Notes

Notes

Notes

Notes

Notes

Notes

Notes

Notes

Notes

Notes

Notes

Notes

Notes

Notes

Made in the USA
Las Vegas, NV
09 December 2021

36770847R10063